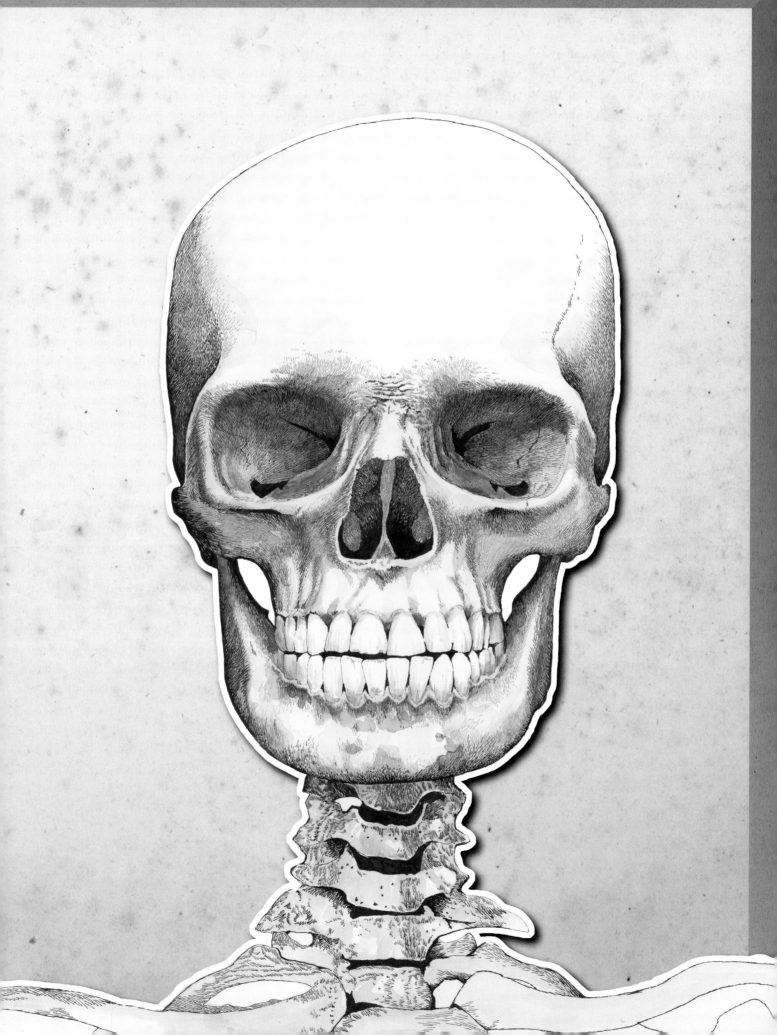

Published by Smart Apple Media,
an imprint of Black Rabbit Books
P.O. Box 3263, Mankato, Minnesota 56002
www.blackrabbitbooks.com

Published by arrangement with
The Salariya Book Company Ltd

Cataloging-in-Publication Data is available
from the Library of Congress

Printed in the United States
At Corporate Graphics,
North Mankato, Minnesota

9 8 7 6 5 4 3 2 1

ISBN: 978-1-62588-340-7

Illustrator: Nicholas Hewetson

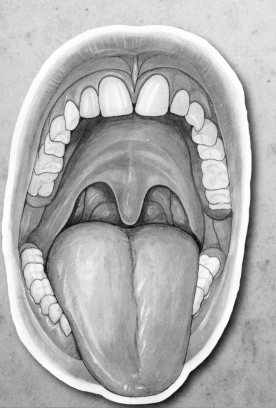

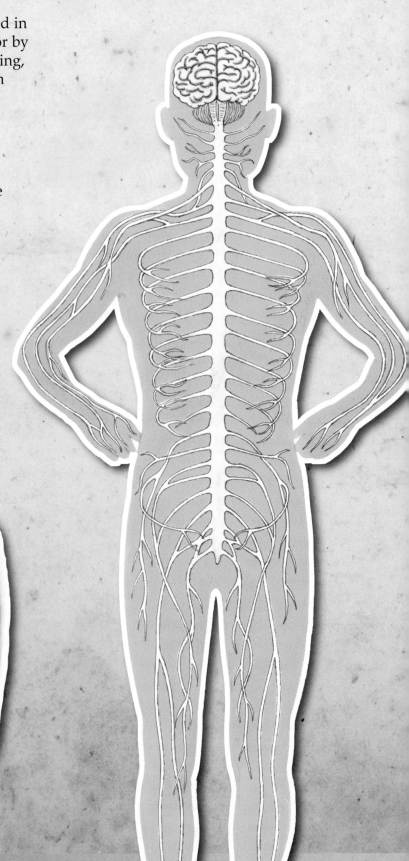

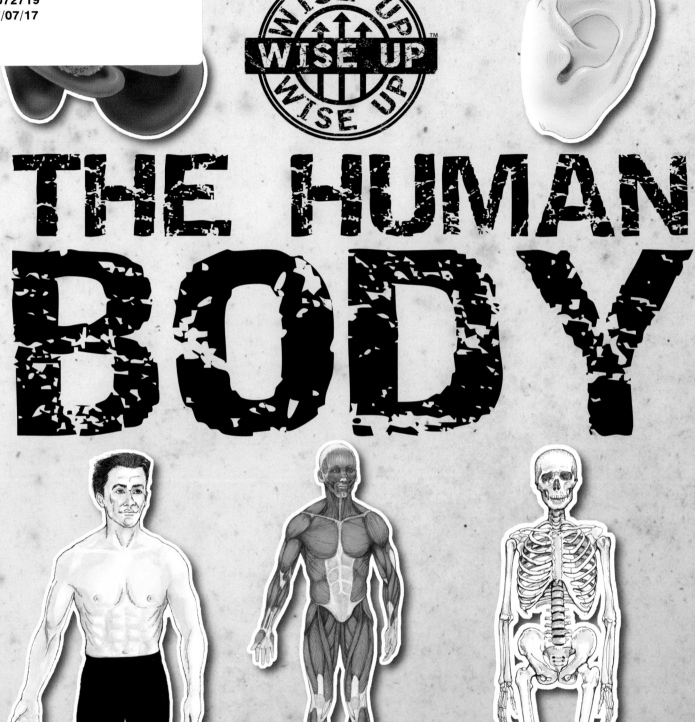

THE HUMAN BODY

Kathryn Senior

A⁺

Smart Apple Media

Contents

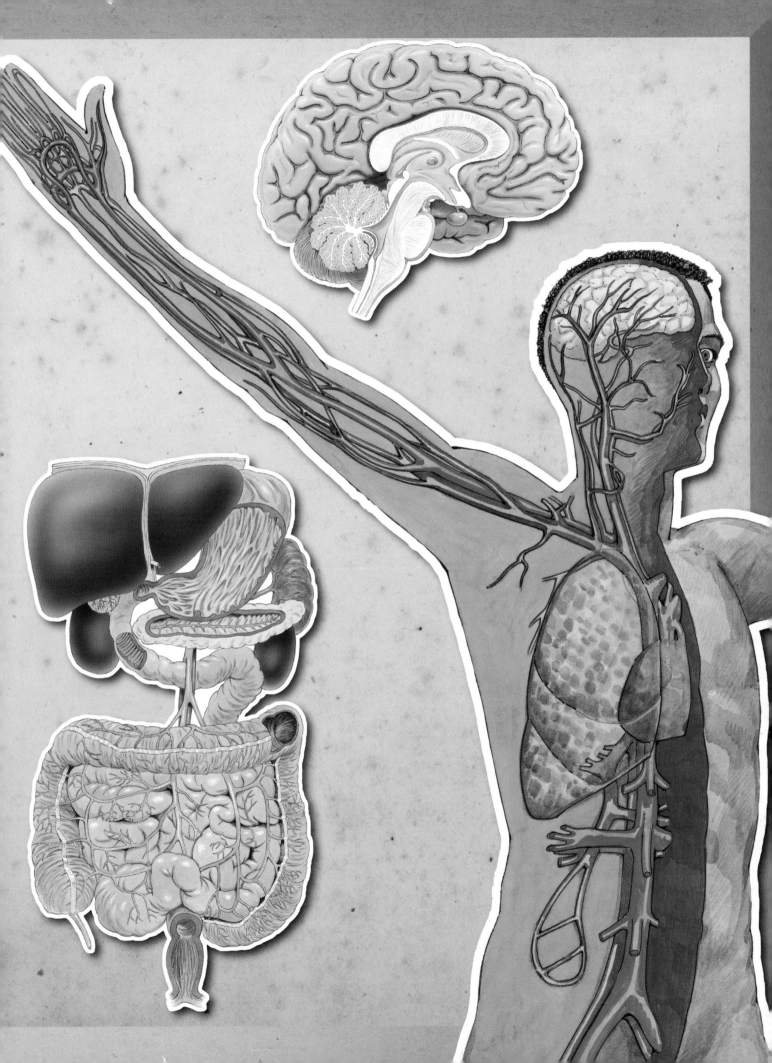

Skin

Skin is the tough, protective wrapping that covers most of the body and stops it from drying out in the sun. It is the body's largest organ and helps to keep its temperature at the right level. When the body gets too hot, sweat glands in the skin release salty water onto the surface. As this evaporates it cools the body down. If the body gets too cold, tiny hairs in the skin stand up and goose bumps appear. These trap a thin layer of air around the body, which stops it from losing heat.

◢ Skin contains many different structures. It has sweat glands to cool the body down and sebaceous glands that produce oil to keep the skin supple.

dermis

sebaceous gland

epidermis

sweat pore

▶ Most of the skin on the body contains small hairs. Only the palms of the hands and the soles of the feet are hair-free.

hair

◣ The epidermis, the outer layer of the skin, is made up of several layers of skin cells. As each layer moves to the surface, it dies and is shed. Only the skin cells in the bottom layers are alive. In this way, a completely new skin is made every three to four weeks.

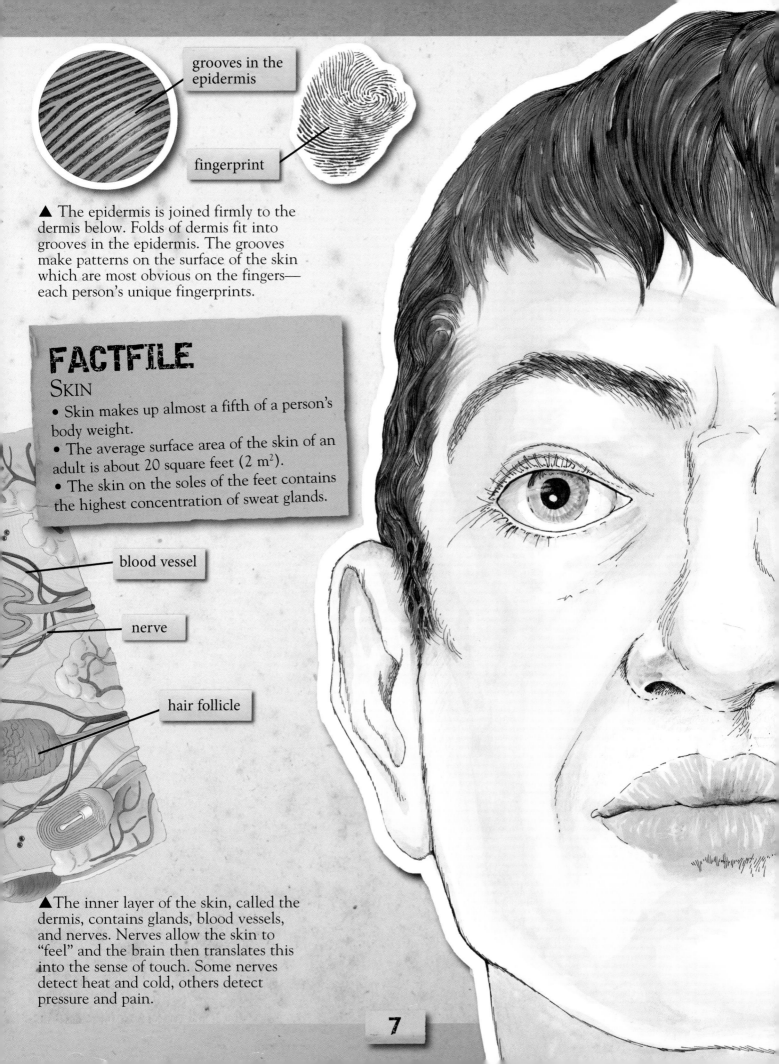

grooves in the epidermis

fingerprint

▲ The epidermis is joined firmly to the dermis below. Folds of dermis fit into grooves in the epidermis. The grooves make patterns on the surface of the skin which are most obvious on the fingers—each person's unique fingerprints.

FACTFILE
SKIN
- Skin makes up almost a fifth of a person's body weight.
- The average surface area of the skin of an adult is about 20 square feet (2 m^2).
- The skin on the soles of the feet contains the highest concentration of sweat glands.

blood vessel

nerve

hair follicle

▲The inner layer of the skin, called the dermis, contains glands, blood vessels, and nerves. Nerves allow the skin to "feel" and the brain then translates this into the sense of touch. Some nerves detect heat and cold, others detect pressure and pain.

Muscles

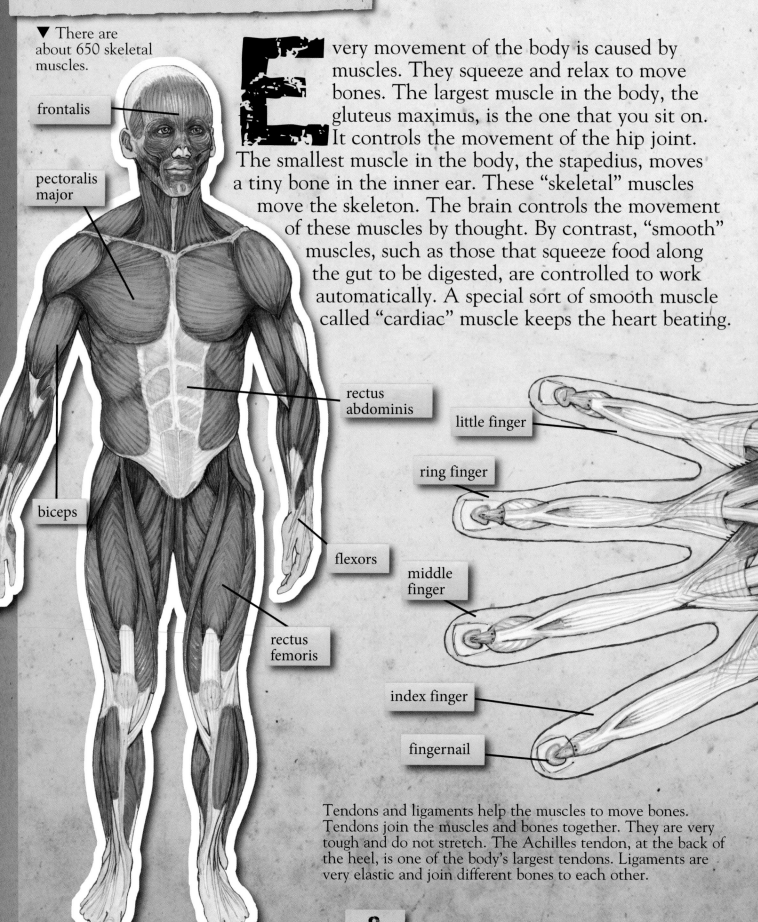

▼ There are about 650 skeletal muscles.

frontalis

pectoralis major

biceps

rectus abdominis

flexors

rectus femoris

little finger

ring finger

middle finger

index finger

fingernail

Every movement of the body is caused by muscles. They squeeze and relax to move bones. The largest muscle in the body, the gluteus maximus, is the one that you sit on. It controls the movement of the hip joint. The smallest muscle in the body, the stapedius, moves a tiny bone in the inner ear. These "skeletal" muscles move the skeleton. The brain controls the movement of these muscles by thought. By contrast, "smooth" muscles, such as those that squeeze food along the gut to be digested, are controlled to work automatically. A special sort of smooth muscle called "cardiac" muscle keeps the heart beating.

Tendons and ligaments help the muscles to move bones. Tendons join the muscles and bones together. They are very tough and do not stretch. The Achilles tendon, at the back of the heel, is one of the body's largest tendons. Ligaments are very elastic and join different bones to each other.

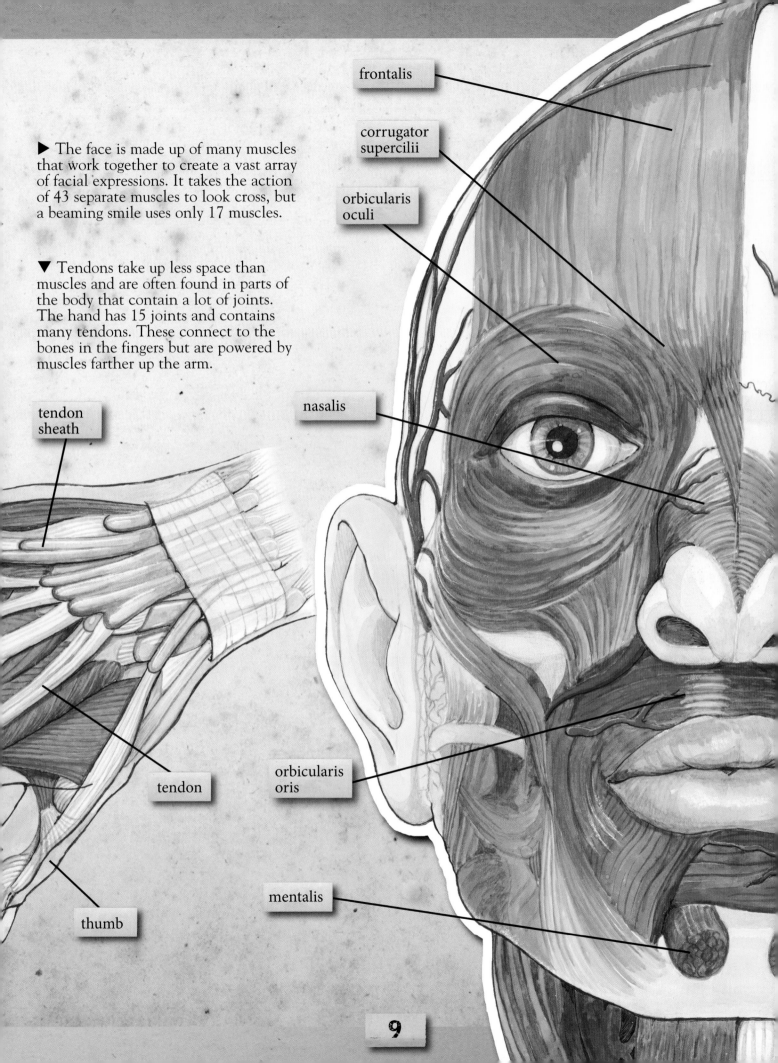

► The face is made up of many muscles that work together to create a vast array of facial expressions. It takes the action of 43 separate muscles to look cross, but a beaming smile uses only 17 muscles.

▼ Tendons take up less space than muscles and are often found in parts of the body that contain a lot of joints. The hand has 15 joints and contains many tendons. These connect to the bones in the fingers but are powered by muscles farther up the arm.

frontalis

corrugator supercilii

orbicularis oculi

nasalis

tendon sheath

tendon

thumb

orbicularis oris

mentalis

Bones

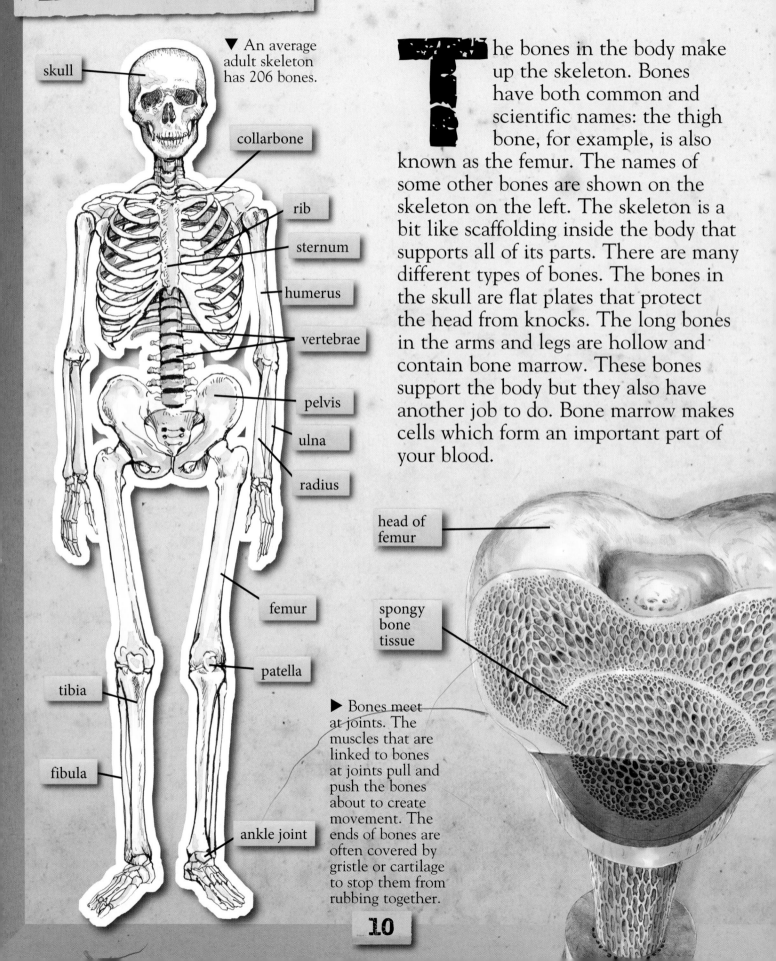

▼ An average adult skeleton has 206 bones.

skull

collarbone

rib

sternum

humerus

vertebrae

pelvis

ulna

radius

femur

patella

tibia

fibula

ankle joint

The bones in the body make up the skeleton. Bones have both common and scientific names: the thigh bone, for example, is also known as the femur. The names of some other bones are shown on the skeleton on the left. The skeleton is a bit like scaffolding inside the body that supports all of its parts. There are many different types of bones. The bones in the skull are flat plates that protect the head from knocks. The long bones in the arms and legs are hollow and contain bone marrow. These bones support the body but they also have another job to do. Bone marrow makes cells which form an important part of your blood.

head of femur

spongy bone tissue

▶ Bones meet at joints. The muscles that are linked to bones at joints pull and push the bones about to create movement. The ends of bones are often covered by gristle or cartilage to stop them from rubbing together.

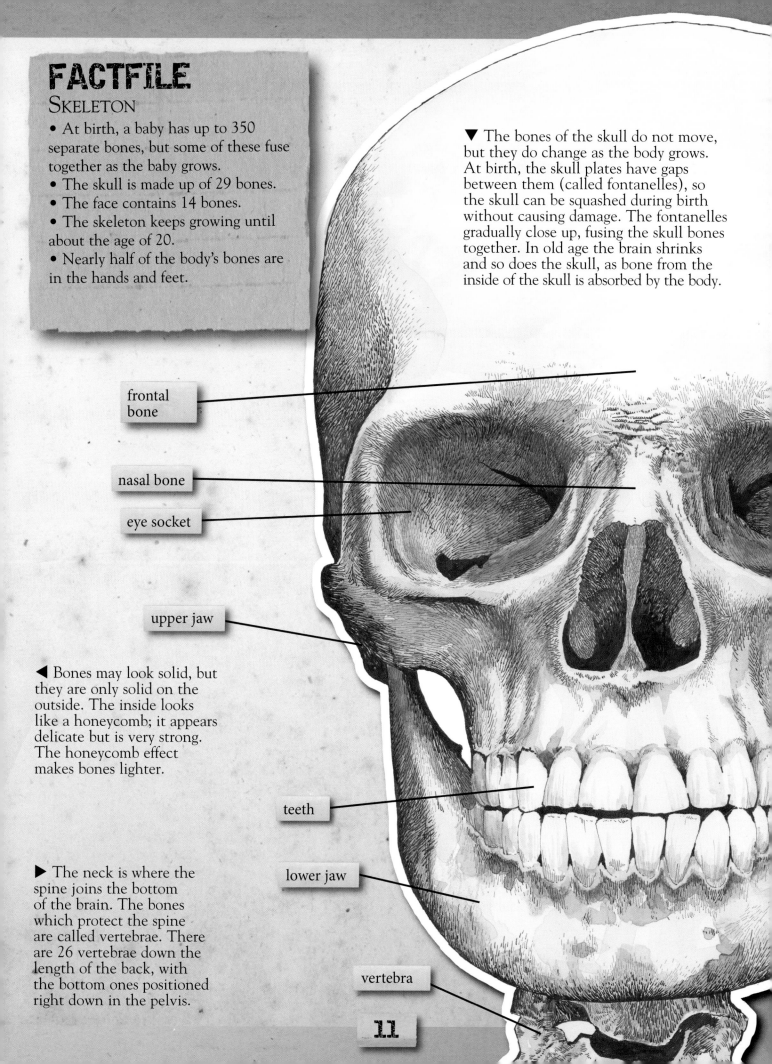

FACTFILE
Skeleton

- At birth, a baby has up to 350 separate bones, but some of these fuse together as the baby grows.
- The skull is made up of 29 bones.
- The face contains 14 bones.
- The skeleton keeps growing until about the age of 20.
- Nearly half of the body's bones are in the hands and feet.

▼ The bones of the skull do not move, but they do change as the body grows. At birth, the skull plates have gaps between them (called fontanelles), so the skull can be squashed during birth without causing damage. The fontanelles gradually close up, fusing the skull bones together. In old age the brain shrinks and so does the skull, as bone from the inside of the skull is absorbed by the body.

frontal bone

nasal bone

eye socket

upper jaw

◄ Bones may look solid, but they are only solid on the outside. The inside looks like a honeycomb; it appears delicate but is very strong. The honeycomb effect makes bones lighter.

teeth

lower jaw

► The neck is where the spine joins the bottom of the brain. The bones which protect the spine are called vertebrae. There are 26 vertebrae down the length of the back, with the bottom ones positioned right down in the pelvis.

vertebra

Heart and Circulation

▶ Some of the waste collected by the blood is taken to the liver to be broken down or to the kidneys to be disposed of in urine.

The heart muscle pumps blood around the body in two main circuits. One circuit is between the heart and the lungs. The other circuit takes blood from the heart to all parts of the body and back again. Blood goes to the lungs to pick up oxygen that our body needs to burn food and to give us energy. Oxygenated blood goes back to the heart and is then pumped out to every part of the body. On its way back, the blood collects carbon dioxide and takes it to the lungs to be exhaled. Blood also collects some other waste products from the body.

▶ A red blood cell is a flattened disk that looks a bit like a flying saucer.

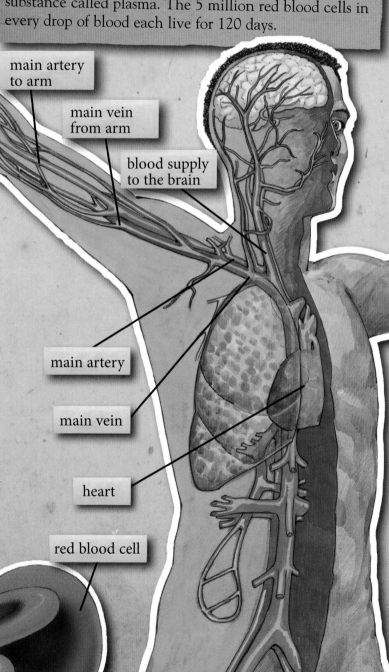

main artery to arm

main vein from arm

blood supply to the brain

main artery

main vein

heart

red blood cell

white blood cell

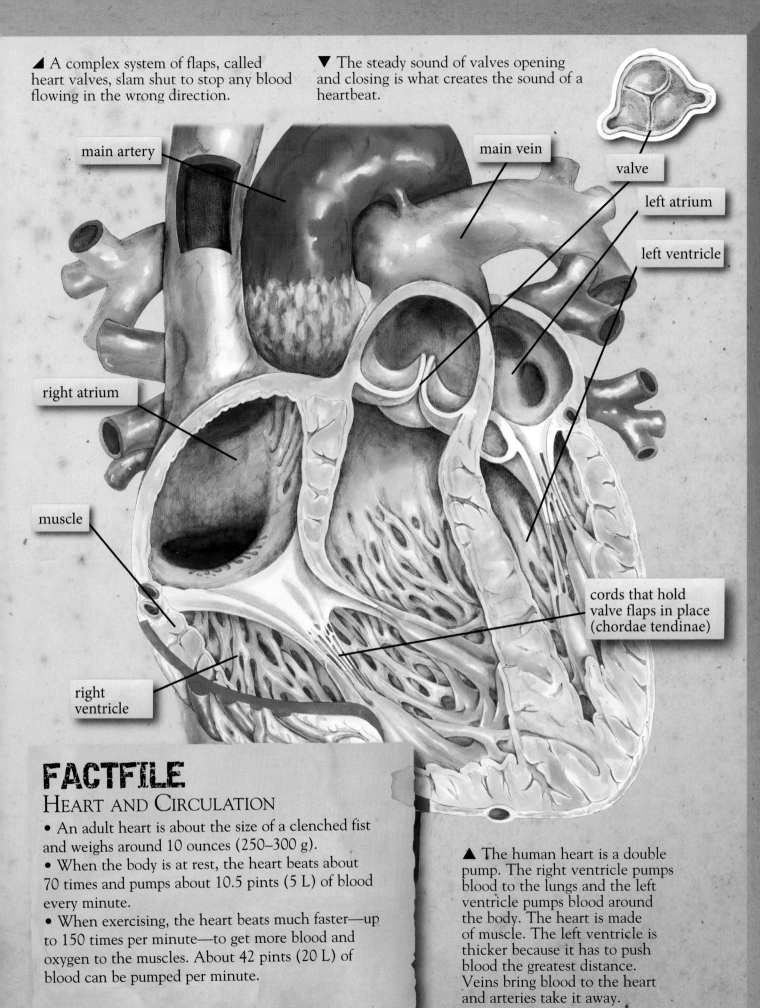

◤ A complex system of flaps, called heart valves, slam shut to stop any blood flowing in the wrong direction.

▼ The steady sound of valves opening and closing is what creates the sound of a heartbeat.

main artery

main vein

valve

left atrium

left ventricle

right atrium

muscle

cords that hold valve flaps in place (chordae tendinae)

right ventricle

FACTFILE
HEART AND CIRCULATION

• An adult heart is about the size of a clenched fist and weighs around 10 ounces (250–300 g).
• When the body is at rest, the heart beats about 70 times and pumps about 10.5 pints (5 L) of blood every minute.
• When exercising, the heart beats much faster—up to 150 times per minute—to get more blood and oxygen to the muscles. About 42 pints (20 L) of blood can be pumped per minute.

▲ The human heart is a double pump. The right ventricle pumps blood to the lungs and the left ventricle pumps blood around the body. The heart is made of muscle. The left ventricle is thicker because it has to push blood the greatest distance. Veins bring blood to the heart and arteries take it away.

Lungs and Breathing

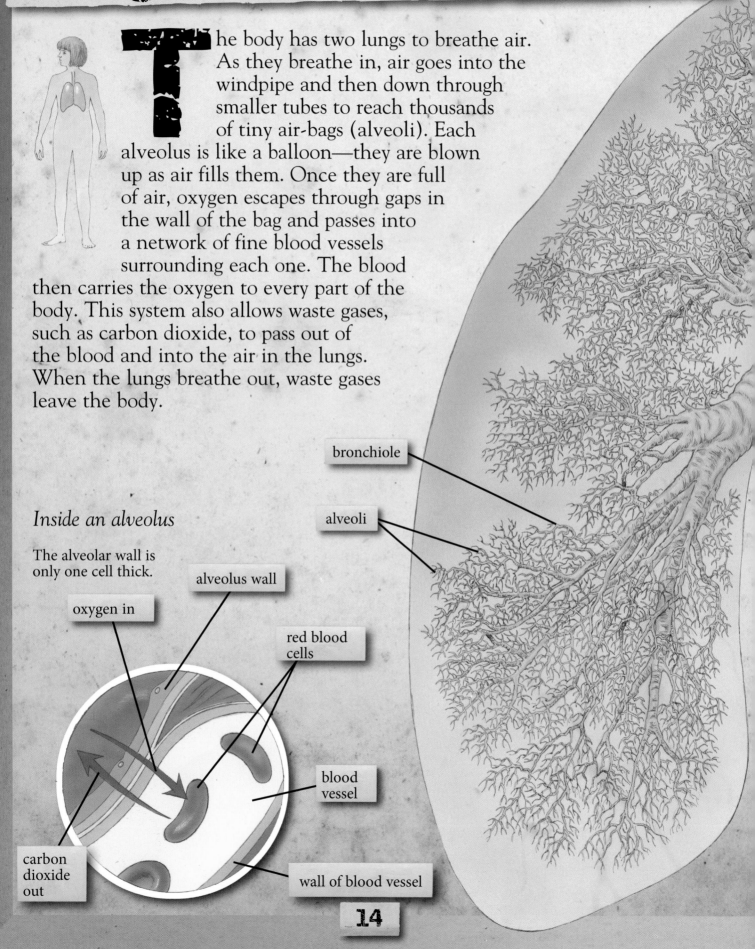

The body has two lungs to breathe air. As they breathe in, air goes into the windpipe and then down through smaller tubes to reach thousands of tiny air-bags (alveoli). Each alveolus is like a balloon—they are blown up as air fills them. Once they are full of air, oxygen escapes through gaps in the wall of the bag and passes into a network of fine blood vessels surrounding each one. The blood then carries the oxygen to every part of the body. This system also allows waste gases, such as carbon dioxide, to pass out of the blood and into the air in the lungs. When the lungs breathe out, waste gases leave the body.

bronchiole

alveoli

Inside an alveolus

The alveolar wall is only one cell thick.

oxygen in

alveolus wall

red blood cells

blood vessel

carbon dioxide out

wall of blood vessel

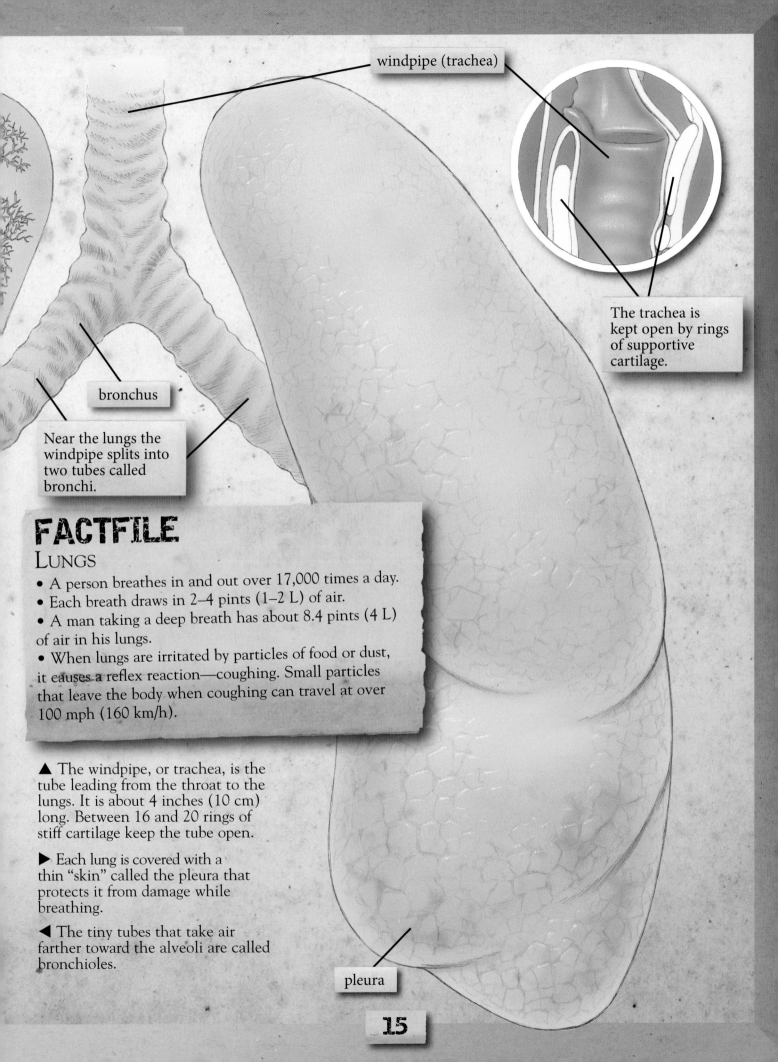

windpipe (trachea)

The trachea is kept open by rings of supportive cartilage.

bronchus

Near the lungs the windpipe splits into two tubes called bronchi.

FACTFILE

LUNGS

- A person breathes in and out over 17,000 times a day.
- Each breath draws in 2–4 pints (1–2 L) of air.
- A man taking a deep breath has about 8.4 pints (4 L) of air in his lungs.
- When lungs are irritated by particles of food or dust, it causes a reflex reaction—coughing. Small particles that leave the body when coughing can travel at over 100 mph (160 km/h).

▲ The windpipe, or trachea, is the tube leading from the throat to the lungs. It is about 4 inches (10 cm) long. Between 16 and 20 rings of stiff cartilage keep the tube open.

▶ Each lung is covered with a thin "skin" called the pleura that protects it from damage while breathing.

◀ The tiny tubes that take air farther toward the alveoli are called bronchioles.

pleura

Eating and Digestion

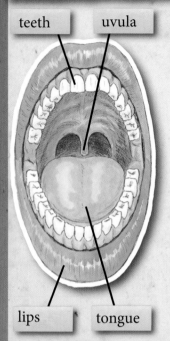

teeth

uvula

lips

tongue

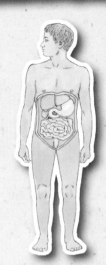

The body needs food to use as fuel. It burns food to get the energy to keep warm, to move, and to think. Without food, the body would eventually die. Food is chewed first, to break it into smaller pieces. When swallowed, it goes down the esophagus and into the stomach. This bag-like organ mixes the food with digestive juices until it turns to mush. It is then squirted into the small intestine to be digested. Useful food substances are taken from the intestine into the blood to be carried to all parts of the body. Any unwanted waste continues through the large intestine and finally leaves the body as feces.

FACTFILE

DIGESTION

• Saliva moistens food so it can be easily swallowed. In a lifetime of 70 years, about 5,300 gallons (20,000 L) of saliva is produced.

• Almost all of the water entering the small intestine every day is taken into the rest of the body.

Surface of stomach

▶ When empty, the stomach is the same size as a large sausage, but it can stretch to the size of a melon.

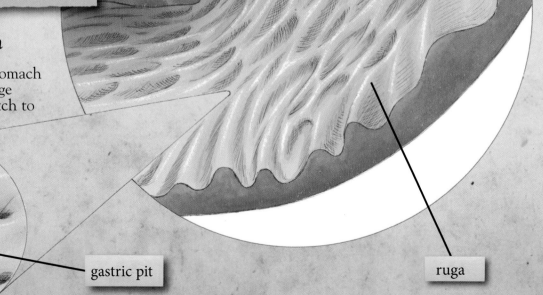

gastric pit

ruga

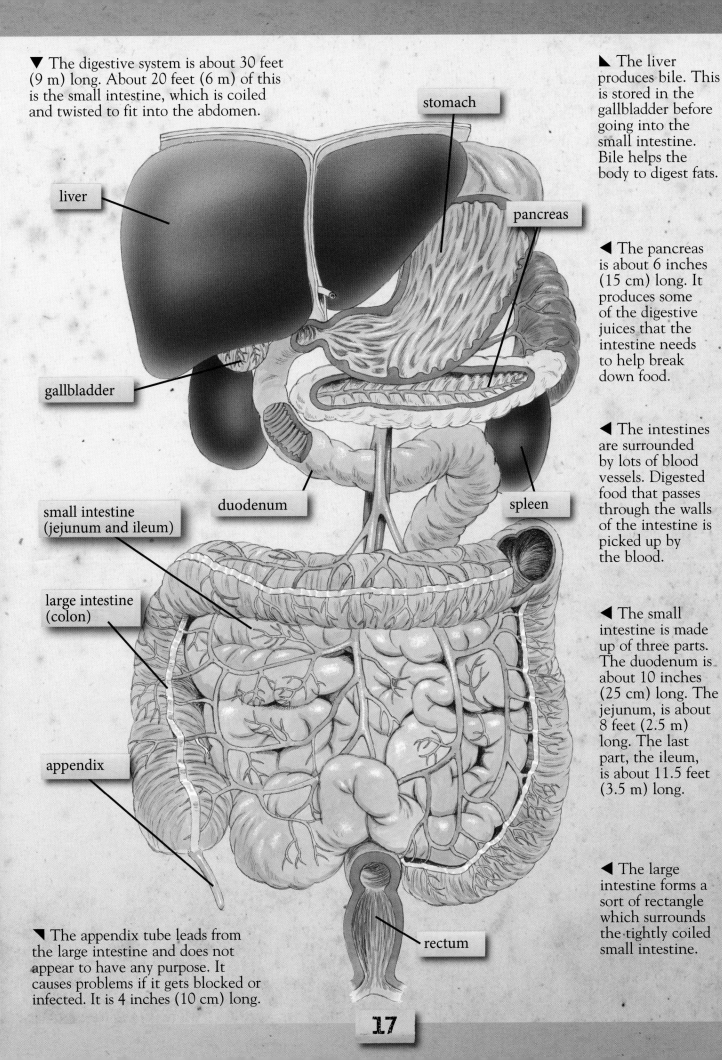

▼ The digestive system is about 30 feet (9 m) long. About 20 feet (6 m) of this is the small intestine, which is coiled and twisted to fit into the abdomen.

◤ The liver produces bile. This is stored in the gallbladder before going into the small intestine. Bile helps the body to digest fats.

stomach

liver

pancreas

◀ The pancreas is about 6 inches (15 cm) long. It produces some of the digestive juices that the intestine needs to help break down food.

gallbladder

duodenum

spleen

◀ The intestines are surrounded by lots of blood vessels. Digested food that passes through the walls of the intestine is picked up by the blood.

small intestine (jejunum and ileum)

large intestine (colon)

◀ The small intestine is made up of three parts. The duodenum is about 10 inches (25 cm) long. The jejunum, is about 8 feet (2.5 m) long. The last part, the ileum, is about 11.5 feet (3.5 m) long.

appendix

rectum

◀ The large intestine forms a sort of rectangle which surrounds the tightly coiled small intestine.

◥ The appendix tube leads from the large intestine and does not appear to have any purpose. It causes problems if it gets blocked or infected. It is 4 inches (10 cm) long.

Kidneys and Liver

Most people have two kidneys, but it is possible to live with only one. The kidneys filter the blood, allowing waste to pass through without losing useful substances such as sugars and water. The waste fluid, or urine, travels down the ureter tube into the bladder. It is stored there until you go to the toilet. Blood is filtered through the kidneys many times each day. As most of the water is taken back into the body, we only produce about 2–4 pints (1–2 L) of urine each day.

▶ The main part of the kidney contains many complicated filters and tubes to remove waste products from the blood that passes through.

▶ The outside of each kidney is protected by a tough capsule.

▼ A large blood vessel called an artery takes blood into the kidney to be cleaned.

▼ A blood vessel called a vein takes the cleaned blood away from the kidney.

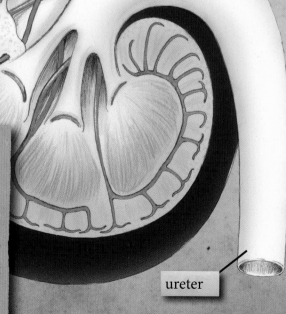

vein

artery

capsule

ureter

▼ A large tube called the ureter joins each kidney to the bladder.

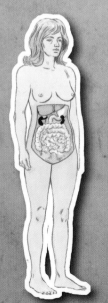

FACTFILE
KIDNEY
- Each kidney is about 6 inches (15 cm) long and weighs about 5 ounces (150 g).
- The kidneys control the amount of water and salt in the body.
- An adult bladder can hold about a pint (0.5 L) before it has to be emptied.

The human liver is a large organ that lies below the lungs and above the stomach and intestines. The liver does many things but it has two main jobs. One is to produce chemicals the body needs, such as hormones and other proteins. It also deals with poisons and wastes within the body. It is the liver that breaks down medicines such as antibiotics and paracetamol. If these substances were not broken down after a few hours, they would do the body more harm than good. The liver also produces a thick green fluid called bile which breaks up fats, making them easier to digest in the stomach and intestine. Bile is stored in the gallbladder.

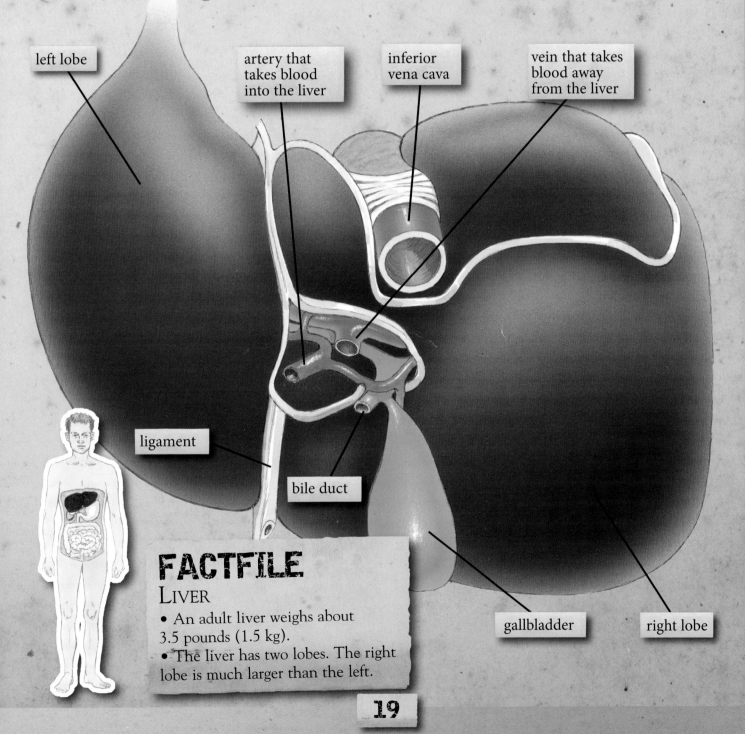

left lobe

artery that takes blood into the liver

inferior vena cava

vein that takes blood away from the liver

ligament

bile duct

gallbladder

right lobe

FACTFILE
LIVER
- An adult liver weighs about 3.5 pounds (1.5 kg).
- The liver has two lobes. The right lobe is much larger than the left.

Brain and Nervous System

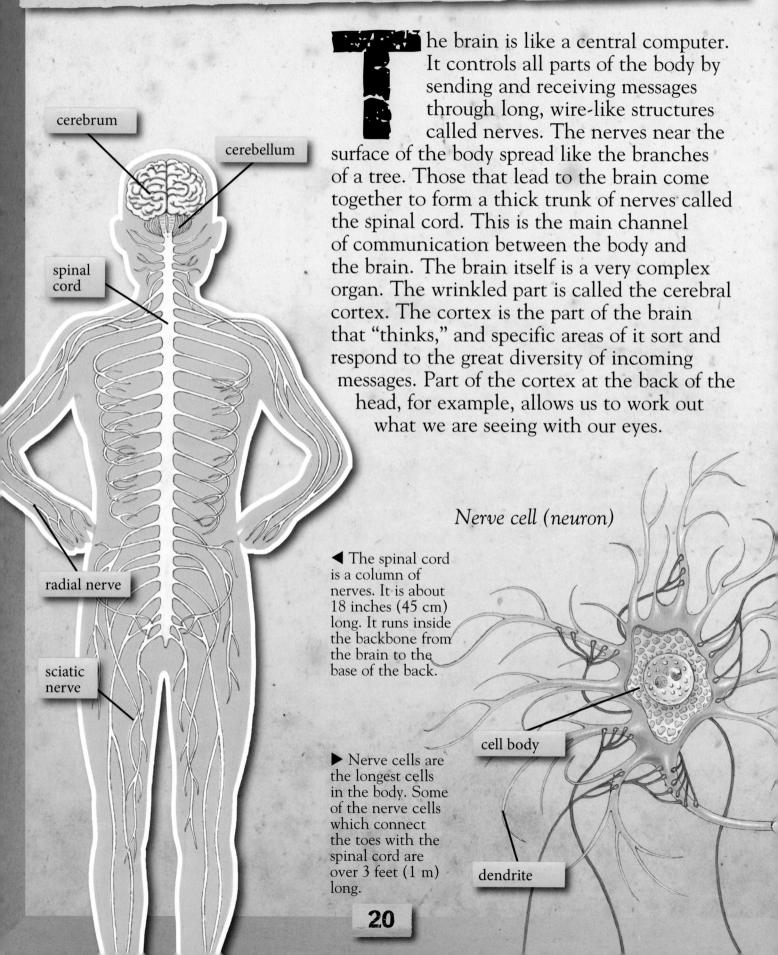

cerebrum

cerebellum

spinal cord

radial nerve

sciatic nerve

The brain is like a central computer. It controls all parts of the body by sending and receiving messages through long, wire-like structures called nerves. The nerves near the surface of the body spread like the branches of a tree. Those that lead to the brain come together to form a thick trunk of nerves called the spinal cord. This is the main channel of communication between the body and the brain. The brain itself is a very complex organ. The wrinkled part is called the cerebral cortex. The cortex is the part of the brain that "thinks," and specific areas of it sort and respond to the great diversity of incoming messages. Part of the cortex at the back of the head, for example, allows us to work out what we are seeing with our eyes.

Nerve cell (neuron)

◄ The spinal cord is a column of nerves. It is about 18 inches (45 cm) long. It runs inside the backbone from the brain to the base of the back.

► Nerve cells are the longest cells in the body. Some of the nerve cells which connect the toes with the spinal cord are over 3 feet (1 m) long.

cell body

dendrite

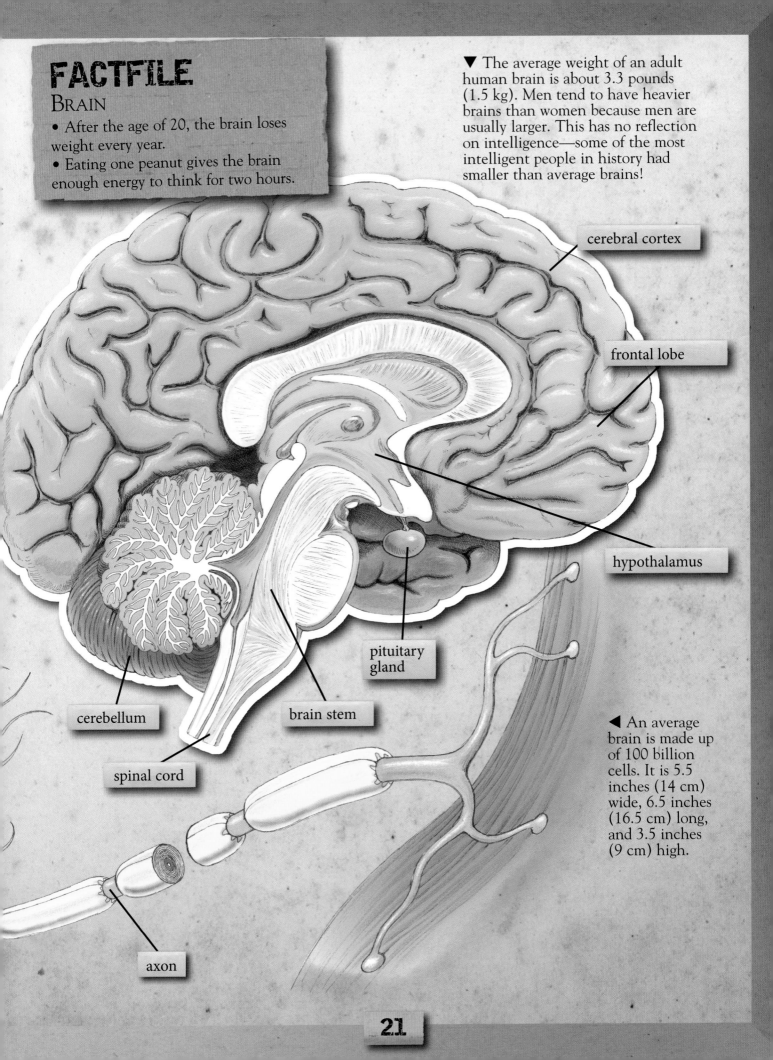

FACTFILE
BRAIN
• After the age of 20, the brain loses weight every year.
• Eating one peanut gives the brain enough energy to think for two hours.

▼ The average weight of an adult human brain is about 3.3 pounds (1.5 kg). Men tend to have heavier brains than women because men are usually larger. This has no reflection on intelligence—some of the most intelligent people in history had smaller than average brains!

cerebral cortex

frontal lobe

hypothalamus

pituitary gland

brain stem

cerebellum

spinal cord

◀ An average brain is made up of 100 billion cells. It is 5.5 inches (14 cm) wide, 6.5 inches (16.5 cm) long, and 3.5 inches (9 cm) high.

axon

Seeing and Hearing

The human head contains two eyes. Each one is shaped like a globe and sits in a socket at the front of the skull, called an orbit. The bone around the orbit surrounds most of the eyeball and protects its delicate parts, so most of the eye is hidden from view. The only visible part is the front of the eyeball with the iris and pupil. The iris is usually colored brown, blue, or green. The pupil is the black center part which changes size: in bright light it gets smaller; in low light it gets bigger.

FACTFILE
EYE
- Light enters the eye through the pupil.
- Light is focused by a lens and forms an image on the retina at the back of the eyeball. This image is converted into an electrical signal that travels along the optic nerve to the brain. The brain decodes the signal and is able to "see" what the eye is looking at.

▶ The outside of the eye is kept moist at all times by tears. The eyelids and eyelashes stop grit and dust from entering the eye. Everyone has a strong blink reflex—automatic shutting of both eyelids—to protect the eyes.

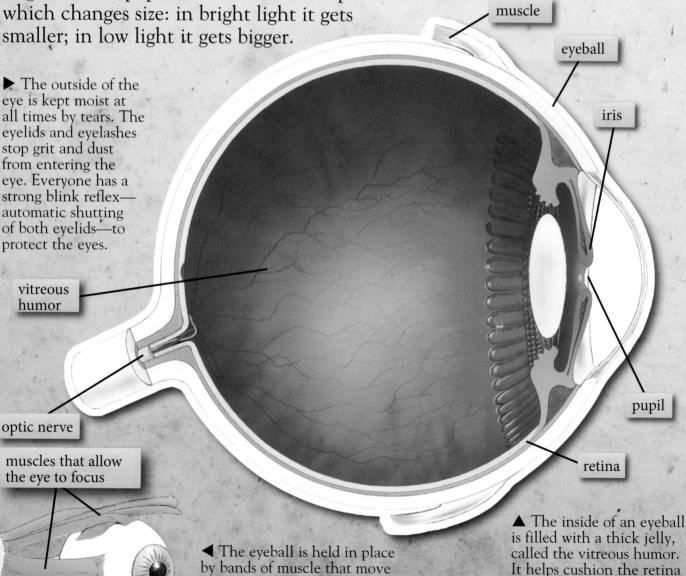

muscle

eyeball

iris

pupil

retina

vitreous humor

optic nerve

muscles that allow the eye to focus

◀ The eyeball is held in place by bands of muscle that move it in so many directions that a lot can be seen without even moving the head.

▲ The inside of an eyeball is filled with a thick jelly, called the vitreous humor. It helps cushion the retina and nerves in the eye so that they are not damaged if the head is bumped.

The external part of the ear, called the pinna, is made of skin and cartilage. It is shaped to gather sound into the ear. An opening in the pinna leads into a complex system of channels and canals that allow hearing and also control the body's sense of balance. Sound waves travel through the bony canal to the eardrum and on into the middle ear where they hit three tiny bones. These bones act as amplifiers, making the original sound 20 times louder. In the inner ear, the amplified sound sets up vibrations in the fluid inside a long, coiled tube called the cochlea. These vibrations cause tiny hairs inside the canal to twitch. The hairs change the sound waves into electrical signals and send them to the brain through the auditory nerve.

Outer ear (pinna)

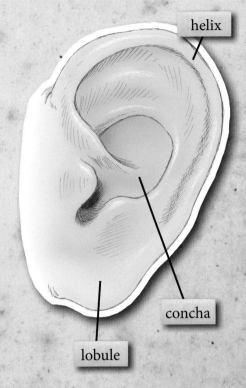

helix

concha

lobule

▼ The fluid inside the cochlea controls your sense of balance. As you move, the fluid in your ear moves too, making the hairs twitch and send signals to the brain. If these signals conflict with those from other senses, such as sight, it can result in a feeling of dizziness or nausea.

cochlea

auditory nerve

the three bones of the middle ear

eardrum

pinna

Eustachian tube

Teeth, Taste, and Smell

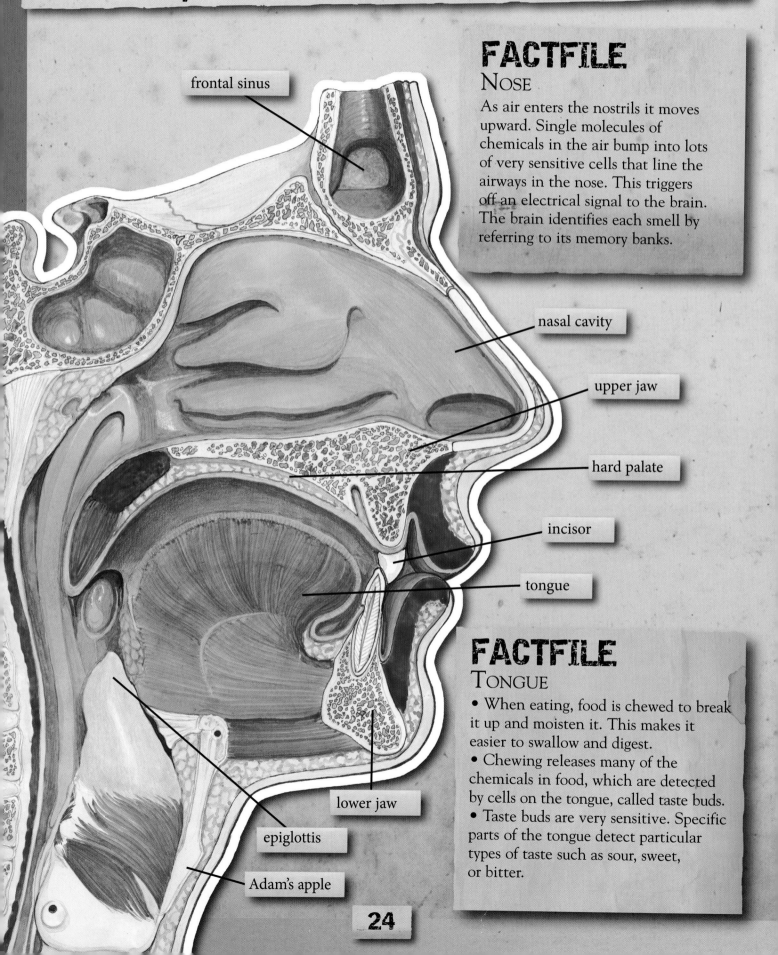

frontal sinus

nasal cavity

upper jaw

hard palate

incisor

tongue

lower jaw

epiglottis

Adam's apple

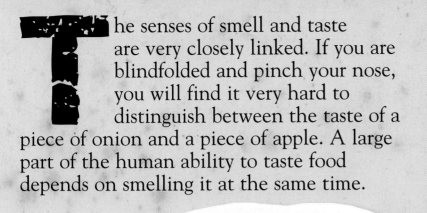

The senses of smell and taste are very closely linked. If you are blindfolded and pinch your nose, you will find it very hard to distinguish between the taste of a piece of onion and a piece of apple. A large part of the human ability to taste food depends on smelling it at the same time.

FACTFILE
TEETH

• A human's first teeth start to grow at about six months old. By the age of two and a half you usually have all your first teeth—the milk teeth. These start to fall out at the age of six or seven and, by the age of 12, most people have 28 adult teeth.

• The last four teeth to appear are the "wisdom" teeth, usually between the ages of 18 and 22.

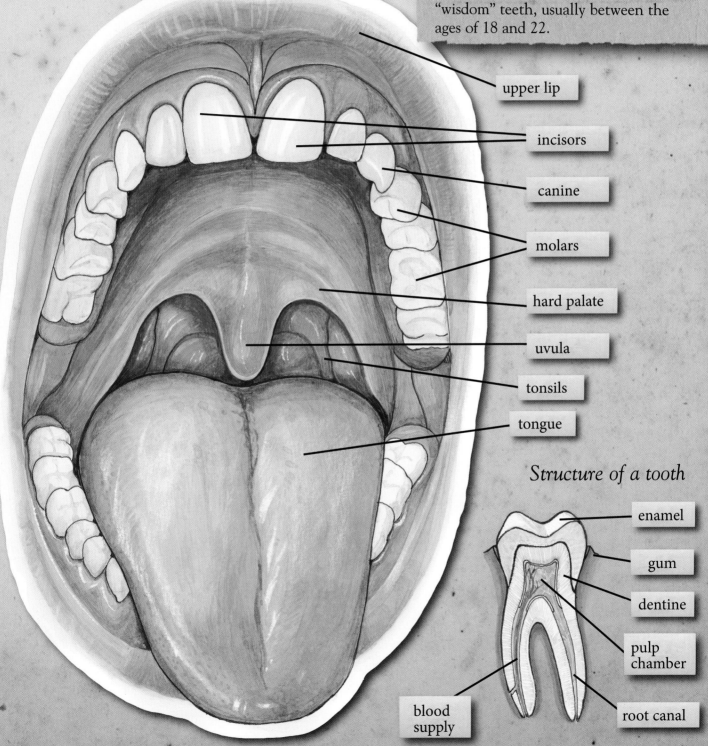

upper lip

incisors

canine

molars

hard palate

uvula

tonsils

tongue

Structure of a tooth

enamel

gum

dentine

pulp chamber

blood supply

root canal

Reproduction

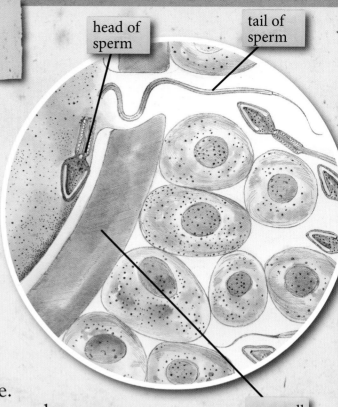

head of sperm

tail of sperm

egg wall

Life starts when a single egg joins with a single sperm. The egg comes from the mother and the sperm from the father. The fertilized egg inside the mother's body then splits into two cells. These cells repeatedly split until the ball of cells begins to resemble a baby.

For the first nine months the baby grows inside the mother's uterus. During this time all the body parts develop until the baby is ready to be born. When the baby is born it is more or less helpless and needs a lot of care. An average newborn baby weighs about 7.5 pounds (3.4 kg). At first the baby drinks only milk, either breast milk or special milk mixed in bottles. Milk contains all the nutrients that the baby needs to grow.

By the age of one, most babies have learned to crawl or shuffle, or even walk. The brain and nerves continue to develop and children gradually become more co-ordinated and able to do things for themselves. The body continues to change and new skills are learned throughout life.

The story of a pregnancy

▼ A woman's body undergoes some remarkable changes when she is pregnant. Before the baby starts to grow, she looks like this.

▼ During the first three months of pregnancy, the baby grows very fast with hardly any outward changes to the mother's body.

▼ After about five months, the baby inside the uterus pushes out from between the intestines and the mother has an obvious "bump."

▼ After seven months the woman looks heavily pregnant and the weight of the baby will be making her feel very tired.

▼ After nine months the woman is very uncomfortable. The baby is so big it squashes her stomach and intestines.

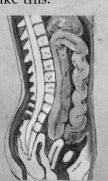
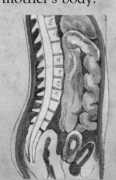
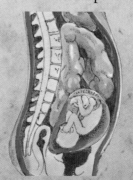
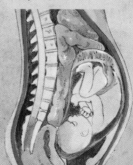
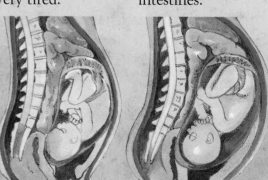

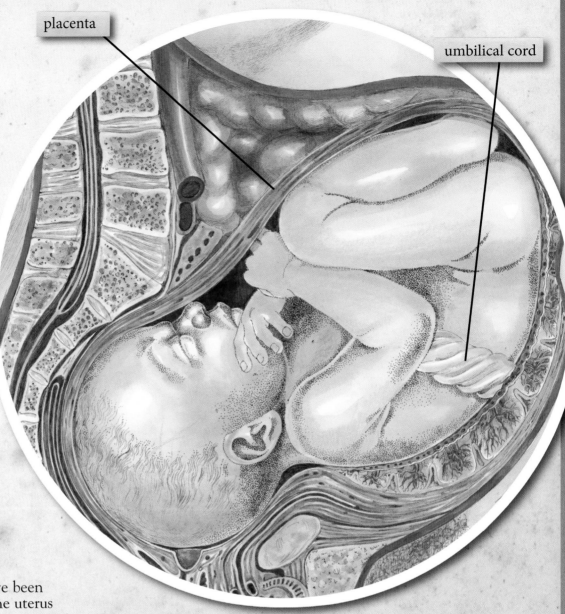

placenta

umbilical cord

▶ After nine months of growing, the baby is very squashed inside its mother's uterus.

▶ The baby gets food and oxygen from its mother through a spongy structure called the placenta.

▶ The placenta is joined to the baby by an umbilical cord. The belly button marks the site of the cord.

▶ The baby usually faces downward as it prepares to be born.

Fiber-optic cameras have been used to film babies in the uterus sucking their thumbs.

FACTFILE
REPRODUCTION

• A normal pregnancy lasts about 266 days from conception to birth.

• As a baby grows it expands its mother's uterus to 1,000 times its non-pregnant volume.

• Every baby starts as a single tiny fertilized egg that is even smaller than a period on this page.

• A new baby is around 20 inches (50 cm) from head to toe.

• A woman who is nine months pregnant has 30 percent more blood than she had before she was pregnant.

Newborn babies fed on milk grow very quickly. By four months, most babies start eating some solid food, too. In its first year, a baby's weight can triple. Most one-year-olds can crawl and some can walk. By the age of four, a child can do many of the things an adult can. Children continue to grow well into their teenage years. Between the ages of 10 and 16, the body starts maturing into its adult form. People tend to wait until their twenties or thirties to start their own family.

▲ Running or jogging strengthens the heart and leg muscles and makes the lungs work harder.

Young babies cannot move in a co-ordinated way—they must learn to sit up, crawl, and walk. As the body matures, such movements become automatic. Running, dancing, and skipping follow on.

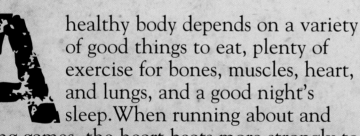

A healthy body depends on a variety of good things to eat, plenty of exercise for bones, muscles, heart, and lungs, and a good night's sleep. When running about and playing games, the heart beats more strongly to get more blood pumping around the body. The more active the muscles are, the more fresh blood they need. When exercising regularly, the heart and muscles get stronger and the body gets fitter. Adults who train very hard build up their muscles. This is at its most extreme in weightlifters. Other sportsmen and sportswomen, such as marathon runners, may look very thin—their strongest muscle is their heart, which does a huge amount of work when they run a 26-mile (42-km) race.

▶ Not being able to sleep when you want to is called insomnia. For most people this happens occasionally, but some people have it every night. They toss and turn and get up feeling tired and irritable because of the lack of much-needed sleep.

A newborn baby sleeps for most of the day, but wakes for milk every two to three hours at first. By the age of six months most babies can sleep for 8 to 12 hours. Children continue to need a lot of sleep until about 10 years old, then they need less. Most adults manage with about seven or eight hours' sleep each night. Older people need even less— perhaps only four or five hours.

Body Quiz

1. **Which is the largest organ in the body?**
   a) The heart
   b) The skin
   c) The brain

2. **What are the structures that join one muscle to another called?**
   a) Ligaments
   b) Tendons
   c) Bones

3. **How many bones are there in an average adult skeleton?**
   a) 206
   b) 306
   c) 350

4. **Which type of blood vessel brings blood to the heart?**
   a) Arteries
   b) White blood cells
   c) Veins

5. **How fast do particles that leave the body in a cough travel?**
   a) 10 mph (16 km/h)
   b) 100 mph (160 km/h)
   c) 1,000 mph (1,600 km/h)

6. **What is the longest part of the small intestine called?**
   a) The duodenum
   b) The jejunum
   c) The ileum

7. **Which one of these jobs is NOT done by the kidneys?**
   a) Controlling the amount of water in the body
   b) Controlling the amount of salt in the body
   c) Controlling the digestion of food

8. **Which are the longest cells in the body?**
   a) Nerve cells
   b) Bone cells
   c) Skin cells

9. **How many senses does the body have?**
   a) 3
   b) 5
   c) 10

10. **What is the structure that joins a baby to its mother before it is born?**
    a) The placenta
    b) The umbilical cord
    c) The uterus

Quiz answers

1) b   see page 6
2) a   see page 8
3) a   see page 10
4) c   see page 13
5) b   see page 15
6) c   see page 17
7) c   see page 18
8) a   see page 20
9) b   see pages 6, 22-25
10) b   see page 27

30

Glossary

abdomen The part of the body between the chest and the pelvis, which contains the intestines and many vital organs.

cardiac The scientific name for anything to do with the heart. Cardiac muscle is the muscle of the heart, and cardiac arrest is when the heart stops beating.

cartilage A spongy material that surrounds the ends of bones where they meet other bones at joints. It protects the ends from rubbing together when they move.

cell The smallest unit of life. Everything in the body is made up of cells or of things produced by cells. Cells in different parts of the body are specialized to do particular jobs. Nerve cells, for example, are long and thin and carry electrical messages.

circulation The way blood travels around the body. It travels through many complicated circuits so that every part of the body constantly receives a supply of fresh blood.

digestion The process that the body uses to break down food. Chemicals are released throughout the digestive system to break down different types of food. The resulting molecules are then taken into the blood and carried around the body. Most digestion happens in the small intestine.

glands Organs that produce chemicals useful to the body. For example, sweat glands in the skin produce sweat, the pancreas produces hormones and chemicals for digestion, and glands in the corner of each eye produce tears.

ligaments The elastic (stretchy) rods that join one bone to another and hold joints together.

nerves Special structures that pass messages around the body. The brain, the center of the nervous system, processes all the messages and controls all the functions of the body.

organ A type of structure in the body that carries out a complicated job. Examples of organs are: the heart, the kidneys, the liver, and the skin. Structures that hold the body together, such as ligaments and cartilage, are not organs.

pregnancy The nine-month period during which a baby grows and develops inside its mother.

skeletal muscle The type of muscle that is joined to the bones of the body and allows movement. This kind of muscle is controlled by thinking about what the body wants to do. For example, to jump up and down, a person consciously moves the muscles in the legs and feet.

smooth muscle The type of muscle that works without the brain consciously thinking about it. Smooth muscles move food along the intestines and keep the heart beating.

tendons Tough, rigid rods that join muscles to bones so that the muscles can move the bones.

waste Any substances that the body does not need. Waste produced by chemical processes in the body is removed from the blood by the "cleaning" action of the kidneys. It then leaves the body in urine. Food waste (what is left after digestion) passes through the large intestine and then leaves the body in the form of feces.

Index